MATH TRAILBLAZERS™

A Mathematical Journey Using Science and Language Arts

Discovery Assignment Book

Grade 1

A TIMS® Curriculum from the
University of Illinois at Chicago

KENDALL/HUNT PUBLISHING COMPANY
4050 Westmark Drive   Dubuque, Iowa 52002

MATH TRAILBLAZERS™

Dedication

This book is dedicated to the children and teachers who let us see the magic in their classrooms and to our families who wholeheartedly supported us while we searched for ways to make it happen.

The TIMS Project

 UIC The University of Illinois at Chicago

This material is based on work supported by the National Science Foundation under grant No. MDR 9050226 and the University of Illinois at Chicago. Any opinions, findings, and conclusions or recommendations expressed in this publication are those of the author(s) and do not necessarily reflect the views of the granting agencies.

Printed in the United States of America
10 9 8 7 6

Table of Contents

Letter to Parents v

Unit 1: **Welcome to First Grade** 1
We're Counting on You! 3
More or Less 5

Unit 2: **Pennies, Pockets, and Parts** 9
Favorite Colors 11
Ten Frames 15
Think and Spin 21
Purchasing with Pennies 27

Unit 3: **Exploring Shapes** 29
Weather 1: Eye on the Sky 31
Describing Shapes 33
Seven Ways to Make a Hexagon 35

Unit 4: **Adding to Solve Problems** 37
Exploring Even and Odd Numbers 39
The Pet Shop 41
Parts and Wholes 43

Unit 5: **Grouping and Counting** 45
Counting by Fives and Tens 47
Sharing Cookies 49

Unit 6: **Measurement: Length** 51
Rolling Along with Links 53
Using Unusual Units 57
Delightful Dachshunds 61
Give 'em an Inch 65

Unit 7: **Patterns and Designs** 69
Pick Apart a Pattern 71
Name Patterns 73
Pattern Block Symmetry 79
Balancing Act 80

Unit 8: **Subtracting to Solve Problems** 81
Our Own Stories 83
Clowning Around 87
How Many in the Bag? 89

Unit 9: **Grouping by Tens** 91
More or Less than 100? 93
Spin for Beans 95
The 50 Chart 99
Measuring with Connecting Links 101

Additional student pages may be found in the *Student Guide, Adventure Book,* or the *Unit Resource Guide.*

Table of Contents

Unit 10: Measurement: Area **103**
Finding Area with Pennies 105
Goldilocks and the Three Rectangles 107
How Much Area? 109
Unit Designs 111

Unit 11: Looking at 100 . . . . **113**
Pennies and Dimes 115
Weather 2: Winter Skies 117

Unit 12: Cubes and Volume **121**
Cubic Classroom 123
TIMS Towers 125

Unit 13: Thinking About Addition and Subtraction **127**
Seeing Doubles 129
Doubles and Halves 131
Problem Solving 139

Unit 14: Exploring Multiplication and Division **141**

Unit 15: Exploring 3-D Shapes **143**
Sizing Cylinders 145
Looking at Prisms 147

Unit 16: Collecting and Organizing Data **151**
The Martians 153
Food Sort 155
Healthy Kids 157

Unit 17: Moving Beyond 100 . . . . **161**
Our Class in Tensland 163
Adding Hundreds 167

Unit 18: Pieces, Parts, and Symmetry **169**
Fold and Color 171
Equal and Unequal 177
Fraction Puzzles 181

Unit 19: Measurement and Mapping **185**
Meet Mr. O and Mr. O's Map 187
Mr. O Left/Right 189

Unit 20: Looking Back at First Grade **191**

Additional student pages may be found in the *Student Guide*, *Adventure Book*, or the *Unit Resource Guide*.

Dear Parents,

MATH TRAILBLAZERS™ is based on the belief that all children deserve a challenging mathematics curriculum and that mathematics is best learned through solving many different kinds of problems. The program provides a careful balance of concepts and skills. Traditional arithmetic skills and procedures are covered through their repeated use in problems and through distributed practice.

MATH TRAILBLAZERS™, however, offers much more. Students using this program will become proficient problem solvers, will know how to approach problems in many different ways, will know when and how to apply the mathematics they have learned, and will be able to clearly communicate their mathematical knowledge. They will learn more mathematics than in a traditional program—computation, measurement, geometry, data collection and analysis, estimation, graphing, patterns and relationships, mental arithmetic, and simple algebraic ideas are all an integral part of the mathematics learned curriculum. They will see connections between the mathematics learned in school and the mathematics used in everyday life. And, they will enjoy and value the work they do in mathematics.

This curriculum was built around national recommendations for improving mathematics instruction in American schools and the research that supported those recommendations. It has been extensively tested with thousands of children in dozens of classrooms over five years of development. **MATH TRAILBLAZERS**™ reflects our view of a complete and well-balanced mathematics program that will prepare children for a world in the 21st century where proficiency in mathematics will be a necessity. We hope that you enjoy this exciting approach to learning mathematics as you watch your child's mathematical abilities grow throughout the year.

Philip Wagreich

Philip Wagreich
Teaching Integrated Mathematics and Science Project
University of Illinois at Chicago
Chicago, Illinois

UNIT 1

Lesson 1 **Look Around You**

Lesson 2 **We're Counting on You!**

Lesson 3 **The Train Game**

Lesson 4 **More or Less**

In My Home

Homework

Dear Family Member:

Your child is learning to count and tally objects. Help your child complete the table below.

Thank you for your cooperation.

Select and count objects such as clocks or shoes around your home. Write or draw each object in the table below. Record the number counted.

Object I Counted	Number

Measuring with Six Links

Compare your chain of six links with objects in the room. Decide if each object is more than, less than, or close to six links. Complete the table.

Object	Circle One
	More Less Close
	More Less Close
	More Less Close
	More Less Close
	More Less Close
	More Less Close

Six Links at Home

Homework

Dear Family Member:

We are studying the ideas of more than, less than, and close to. Please help your child complete the table below.

Thank you for your cooperation.

Write or draw five household objects in the table below. After comparing the lengths of these objects with the picture of six links on the right, circle "more," "less," or "close."

Object	Circle One
	More Less Close
	More Less Close
	More Less Close
	More Less Close
	More Less Close

UNIT 2

Lesson 1   **Favorite Colors**   DAB

Lesson 2   **Ten Frames**   DAB

Lesson 3   **Think and Spin**   DAB

Lesson 4   **Pockets Graph**   URG

Lesson 5   **Pocket Parts**   SG

Lesson 6   **What's in that Pocket?**   SG

Lesson 7   **Purchasing with Pennies**   DAB

Name _____ Date _____

Kitchen Tools

Homework

Dear Family Member:

We have been thinking about numbers and tallies. Please help your child count and tally the objects below.

For example: $\text{卌} \, \text{II}$ for seven

You might ask questions that will stimulate your child's thinking:
* How many plates and forks are there all together?
* How many more cups than forks are there?

Count and tally the objects in the table.

Objects	Tallies	Total

House Walk

Homework

Dear Family Member:

Please help your child count the objects listed in the table. As you go from room to room, have your child record a tally for each object he or she sees. After all of the rooms have been checked, have your child count the tallies and record the total.

Thank you for your cooperation.

Record a tally for each object in your home. Then, count the tallies and record the total.

Object	Tallies	Total
Lamp		
Chair		
Table		
Clock		
Window		

Empty Ten Frames

What's My Number?

Write the number of counters in each ten frame on the line.

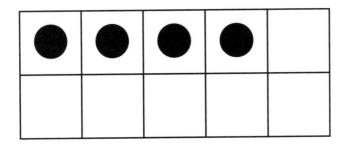

_____

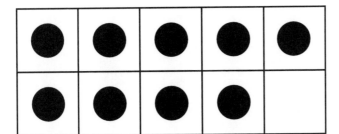

_____

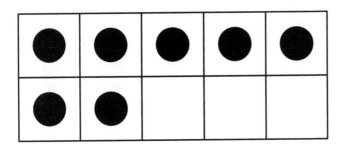

_____

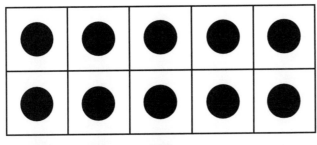

_____

What's My Sentence?

Write a number sentence for each ten frame.

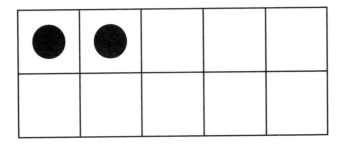

$\boxed{} + \boxed{} = \boxed{}$

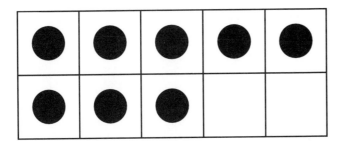

$\boxed{} + \boxed{} = \boxed{}$

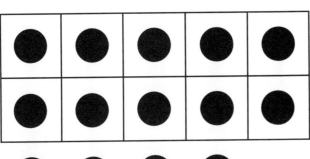

$\boxed{} + \boxed{} = \boxed{}$

$\boxed{} + \boxed{} = \boxed{}$

Think and Spin

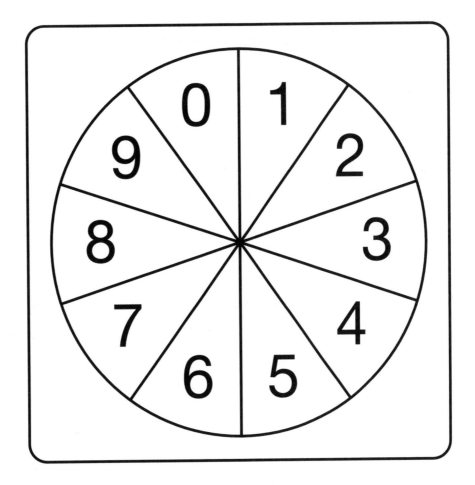

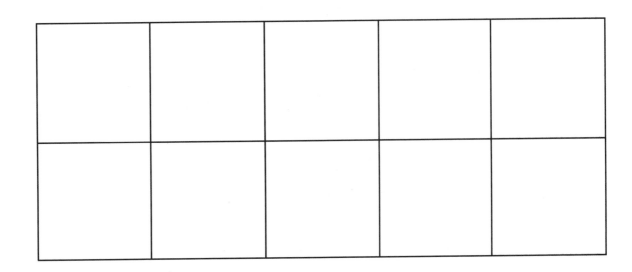

Ten Frame Recording Sheet

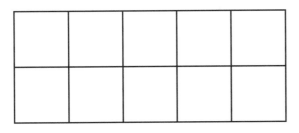

_____

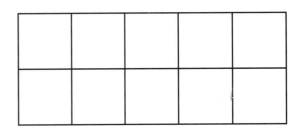

_____

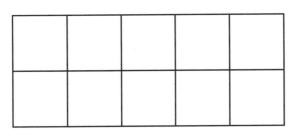

_____

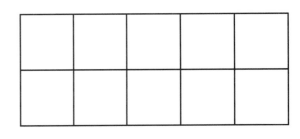

_____

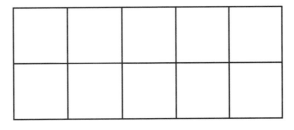

_____

Think and Spin at Home

Homework

Dear Family Member:

Your child completed the *Think and Spin* Activity in math class. Please ask him or her to tell you the steps. In case he or she has trouble, here are some guidelines.

1. Spin the spinner. Use a pencil and a paper clip or a bobby pin as a spinner.

2. Record the number on a ten frame.

3. Write a number sentence under the ten frame.

Thank you for your cooperation.

Play Think and Spin with a family member.

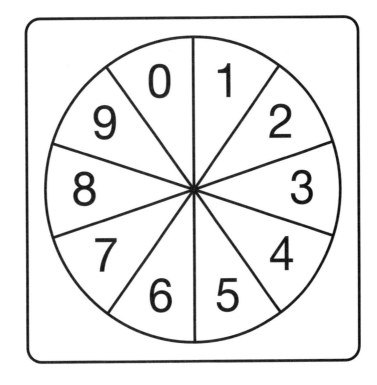

What Would I Buy?

Homework

Dear Family Member:

Look at the items below with your child. Ask him or her to read the price for each item. Assist your child with the reading of each question. While your child is deciding which items to circle, encourage him or her to use the pennies. To answer Question 2, invite your child to draw a picture or use a number sentence (for example, 5¢ + 3¢ = 8¢). If your child is ready, ask the same questions with fifteen pennies.

Thank you for your cooperation.

Look at the items below.

1. Circle the items you would buy if you had ten pennies. (If you want two of the same item, make two circles around it.)

2. How much would you pay for all the items you circled? Show how you found your answer.

_____

3. Would you have any pennies left over? How many?

_____

UNIT 3

Lesson 1	**Weather 1: Eye on the Sky**	
Lesson 2	**Shapes around Us**	
Lesson 3	**Describing Shapes**	
Lesson 4	**Seven Ways to Make a Hexagon**	
Lesson 5	**How Many Does It Take?**	
Lesson 6	**Mystery Figure**	

Name _____ Date _____

Weather Calendar

Time of Day: 🕐   Month: _____   Year: _____

Sunday	Monday	Tuesday	Wednesday	Thursday	Friday	Saturday

Nancy's Apartment and Yard

Homework

Find all the shapes below.

Outline all △**'s with red,** □**'s with blue,** ○**'s with green, and** ▭**'s with yellow.**

How many of each shape do you see?

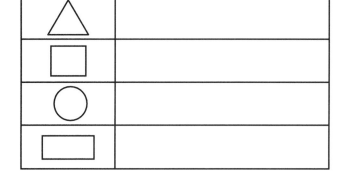

First Grade Times

First Graders Find Seven Ways to Make a Hexagon

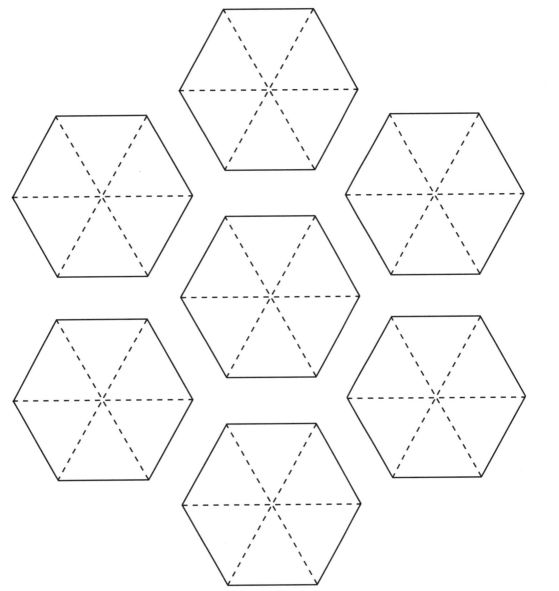

UNIT 4

Lesson 1   **Exploring Even and Odd Numbers**

Lesson 2   **The Pet Shop**

Lesson 3   **Parts and Wholes**

Lesson 4   **Counting On to Add**

Even or Odd?

1. Write a number for each picture.

_____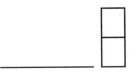

_____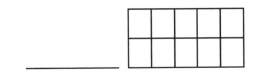

_____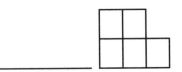

_____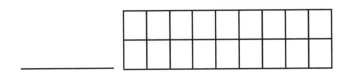

_____

_____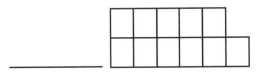

_____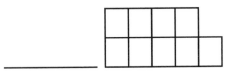

_____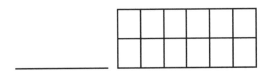

_____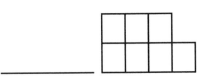

_____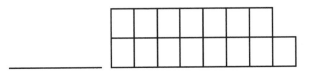

2. Circle the even numbers.

3. Look at the pictures above. Which numbers are odd?

_____

Is My Home Even or Odd?

Homework

Example:

The number seven is odd because there is one leftover.

A number such as six is even because there are no leftovers.

Object	Number of Objects in My Home	Even or Odd
Chairs		Even or Odd
Rugs		Even or Odd
Lamps		Even or Odd
Tables		Even or Odd
Shoes		Even or Odd
Spoons		Even or Odd

Animal Addition Stories

Homework

Example:

Janice has two dogs and three cats in her home. She has five pets in all. (2 + 3 = 5)

Write an addition story about animals. Draw a picture about your story.

Addition Story:

_____

_____

_____

_____

Picture:

Parts and Wholes

I am showing different ways to make _____ .

✂ -

Part   **Part**

_____ + _____ = _____

✂ -

Part   **Part**

_____ + _____ = _____

✂ -

Part   **Part**   **Part**

_____ + _____ + _____ = _____

✂ -

Part   **Part**   **Part**

_____ + _____ + _____ = _____

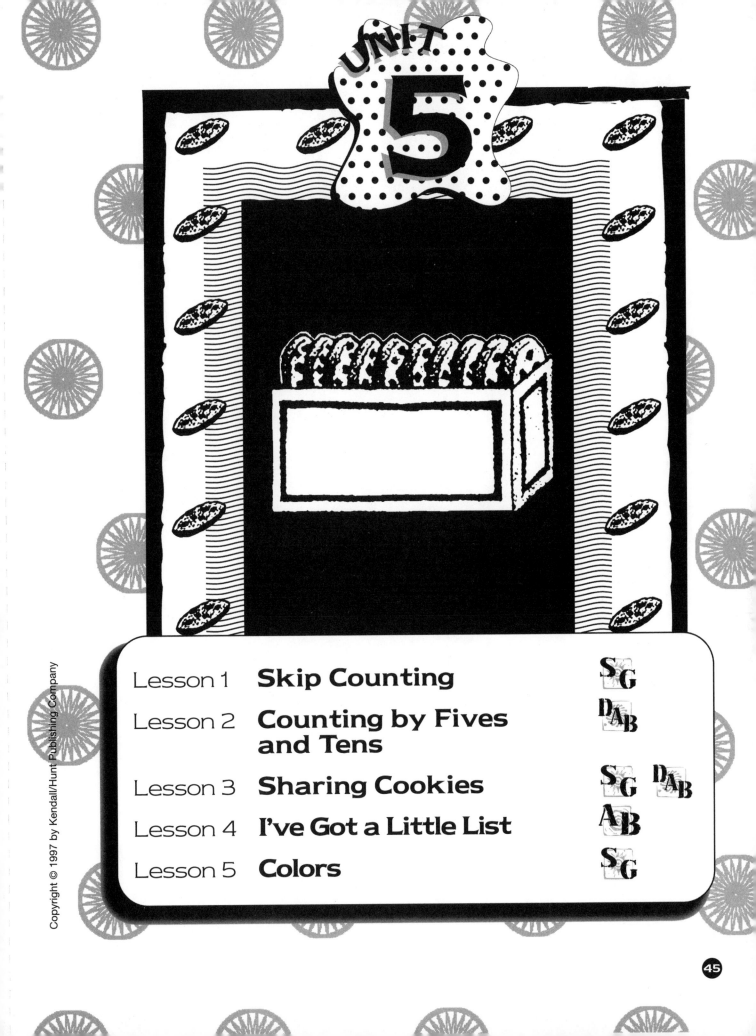

UNIT 5

Lesson 1 **Skip Counting**   S G

Lesson 2 **Counting by Fives and Tens**   D A B

Lesson 3 **Sharing Cookies**   S G   D A B

Lesson 4 **I've Got a Little List**   A B

Lesson 5 **Colors**   S G

Ten Frames

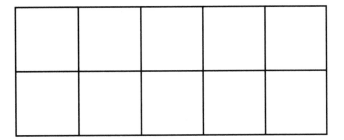

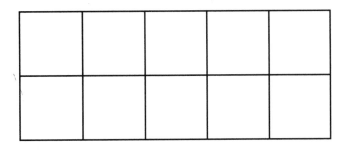

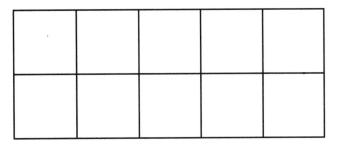

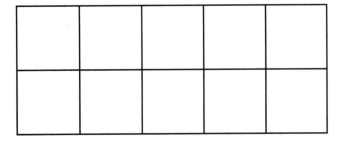

Cookie Factory

Homework

Count, group, and box the cookies. Record your answers below.

	Number of Cookies	Boxes	Leftover Cookies
Work Slip	22		
Work Slip	26		
Work Slip	35		
Work Slip	39		
Work Slip	50		

UNIT 6

Lesson 1 **Linking Up**

Lesson 2 **Rolling Along with Links**

Lesson 3 **Betty Builds a Better Racer**

Lesson 4 **Using Unusual Units**

Lesson 5 **Delightful Dachshunds**

Lesson 6 **Give 'em an Inch**

51

Two Car Roll-off

Homework

Two cars rolled from two ramps. In the drawing below, you are seeing the tops of the cars from above.

1. How far did car A roll? _____

2. How far did car B roll? _____

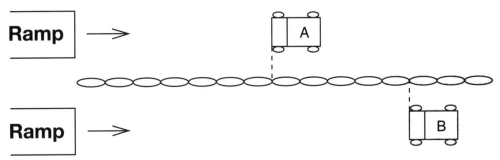

3. How much farther did car B roll than car A?

_____

4. Why do you think car B rolled farther?

_____

_____

_____

Name _____   Date _____

Brian's Class

Brian's class found the data shown in the graph below.

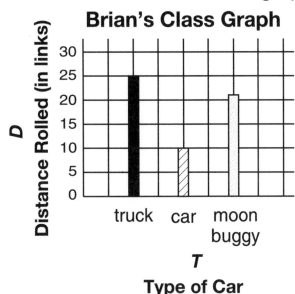

1. Which car was the best roller?

_____

2. Which car was the worst roller?

_____

3. How much farther did the truck travel than the car?

_____

4. About how far did the moon buggy roll?

_____

5. How much farther would the truck have to roll to reach a distance of 30 links?

_____

Measuring at Home

Homework

Dear Family Member:

The boy in the picture is measuring a bed. He is using the edge of a paper towel as a unit. Help your child measure four things in your home using one object as the unit of measure. Some objects you might use are a cooking tool, a cereal box, a pencil, or a book.

Record your data in the table below.

Four Things Measured at Home

Things I Measured	Length Measured Using _____

Stepping Out with My Family

Homework

Dear Family Member:

Your child used footsteps to measure distances in the classroom. Encourage your child to measure straight distances in your home by counting his or her steps as he or she walks "heel-to-toe." For example, your child might walk from the refrigerator to the kitchen table. Invite your child to write or draw pictures in the "From" and "To" columns to indicate the distances measured. After your child measures and records the distances, ask him or her to predict the measurement if your footsteps were used. Check your child's prediction by measuring each distance using your footsteps. Ask your child to record your measurements.

Choose distances in your home, measure them, and record the data in the table below.

Distances in My Home

From	To	Number of My 👣	Number of Your 👣

Darling Dogs

Homework

Dear Family Member:

In class your child is learning to compare lengths. Help him or her complete the following problems. Encourage your child to use the objects mentioned, if they are available, to help him or her solve the problems.

Use measurement tools to answer the questions below.

1. A poodle named Lady is 10 spoons long. Her friend Buddy, a dachshund, is 25 keys long. Which dog is longer?

_____

2. Twelve puppies are waiting in line for baths. The line is 100 keys long. Four Dobermans are waiting in line to get their nails clipped. Their line is 40 pens long. Which line is longer?

_____

3. Chopper, a German shepherd, is 46 pennies long. Indie, a husky, is 43 nickels long. Which dog is longer?

_____

Comparing Links and Cubes

Predict the longer length. Compare chains to measure. Then, circle the longer one.

Prediction		Actual	

A.    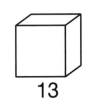   

     9   13   9   13

B.   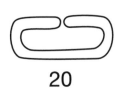

     20   20   20   20

C. 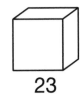   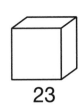   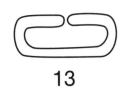

     13   23   13   23

D. Write the lengths in order from shortest to longest.

Shortest

_____   _____   _____

_____   _____   _____

Longest

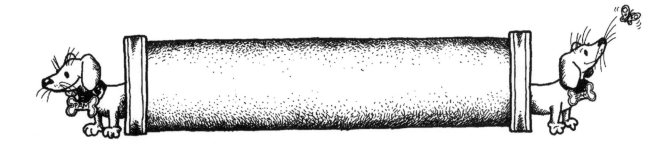

Using Inches to Measure

Cut out the ruler strip and the inch boxes below.

Start →

← Stop

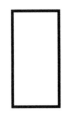

Could Be or Crazy?

Read each of the measurements below. Decide whether each one seems possible or crazy. Circle your answer. Use your 8-inch ruler to help you decide.

1. A big toe is 5 inches long.

could be   or   crazy

2. My teacher's foot is 10 inches long.

could be   or   crazy

3. The length of a pencil is 20 inches.

could be   or   crazy

4. The height of Bessie's doll is 25 inches.

could be   or   crazy

5. Name something that could be 50 inches long.

_____

6. For what object is 50 inches a crazy measurement?

_____

UNIT 7

Lesson 1 **Line Up!**

Lesson 2 **Pick Apart a Pattern**

Lesson 3 **Name Patterns**

Lesson 4 **Pattern Block Symmetry**

Lesson 5 **Balancing Act**

Twins

Write A, B, or C on the line under each object to show the pattern. Draw a ring around the repeating pattern unit.

1.

_____

2.

_____

3.

_____

4.

_____

Name Grid

Create a name grid pattern using your first name. Write one letter of your name in each box. Color the last letter of your name each time it occurs. Be careful not to skip any boxes.

Ten-by-Ten Name Grid

Homework

Dear Family Member:

Your child is learning about patterns in class. Help him or her create a name-grid pattern. Your child should fill in the grid by writing his or her first name many times. One letter of the name should be written in each box. Have your child color the last letter of his or her first name each time it occurs. Be careful not to skip any boxes.

Write your first name repeatedly in the boxes below.

Names and Grids

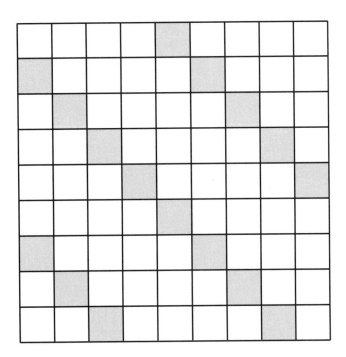

1. Circle the name that fits the pattern on this grid.

Maggie

Lynne

Van

Miko

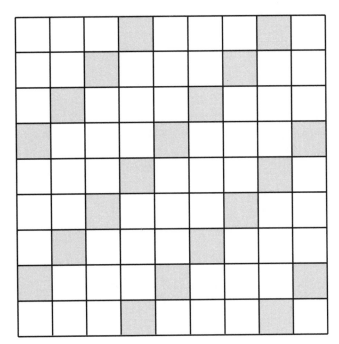

2. Write a name that fits the pattern on this grid.

_____

Tree

1. Cover this side.

2. Make this side balance.

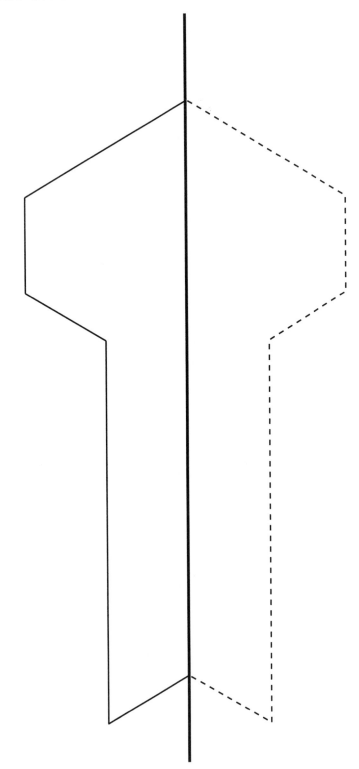

Balancing Act

Use pattern blocks to balance designs below.

UNIT 8

Lesson 1 **At the Circus**

Lesson 2 **Our Own Stories**

Lesson 3 **Clowning Around**

Lesson 4 **How Many in the Bag?**

Lesson 5 **Making Flip Books**

Whole-Part-Part Mat

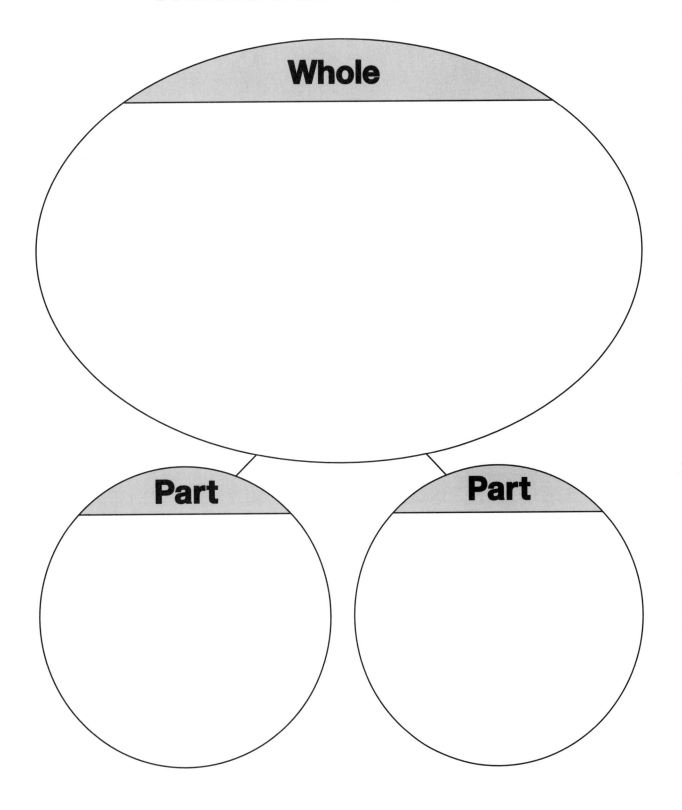

H☺mewⓞrk

Subtraction Story

_____ – _____ = _____
   whole   *part*   *part*

Taking Home Subtraction Cartoons
Homework

Dear Family Member:

Your child illustrated a subtraction cartoon in class. Encourage your child to illustrate another subtraction story based on a subtraction number sentence. Help your child choose an appropriate number sentence such as $9 - 4 = 5$ or $12 - 3 = 9$. Please ask your child to read the subtraction sentence and tell the story that he or she illustrates. You can help your child by asking him or her to identify the whole, the part that is taken away, and the part that is left.

Please send the subtraction cartoon story to school tomorrow so that your child can share it with the class.

Thank you for your cooperation.

_____ − _____ = _____

Counting Up at Home

Homework

Dear Family Member:

In class, your child has been playing *How Many in the Bag?* with a partner. We would like you to play this game with your child. To play, you will need a bag and 20 beans (or other objects).

1. Put between 10 and 20 beans (or other objects) in a bag. Write the number of objects on the bag.

2. Pull out at least half of the beans, and place them on the table. Ask your child to count them.

3. Without looking in the bag, your child should figure out how many beans are left in the bag.

4. He or she should record the number sentence for this problem on the lines provided below and on the following page.

5. Repeat this activity at least three times.

Ask your child how he or she found the answer. Children use many strategies for solving problems. One strategy often used by young children is called "counting up." For example, if there are 14 beans in the bag and 11 are taken out, the child might count from 11 to 14 to find how many are left in the bag: "12, 13, 14." Since three more were counted, three is the answer.

Thank you for your cooperation.

_____ − _____ = _____
  in the bag   *taken out*   *left in the bag*

_____ − _____ = _____
  in the bag   *taken out*   *left in the bag*

_____ – _____ = _____
in the bag   *taken out*   *left in the bag*

_____ – _____ = _____
in the bag   *taken out*   *left in the bag*

24   18   27

Lesson 1   **Spill the Beans**

Lesson 2   **More or Less than 100?**

Lesson 3   **Spin for Beans**

Lesson 4   **The 50 Chart**

Lesson 5   **The 100 Chart**

Lesson 6   **Measuring with Connecting Links**

Lesson 7   **Numbers in the News**

Lesson 8   **Full of Beans**

Lesson 9   **Maria's Marble Mart**

How Many Letters?

Homework

Write the number of letters in the first names of four people and/or pets at home.

First Name	Number of Letters

Total Number of Letters = _____

Draw a picture or tell how you found the total number of letters.

Return this sheet to school by _____ .

Spin for Beans 100 Playing Mat

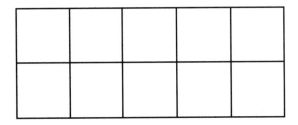

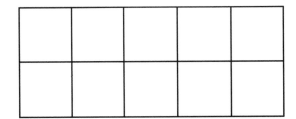

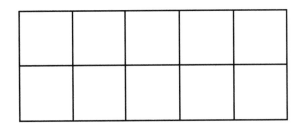

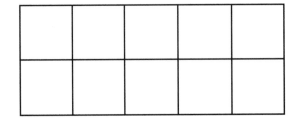

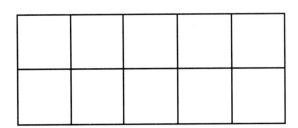

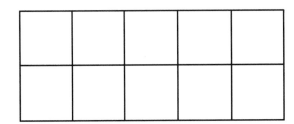

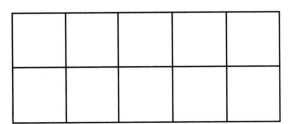

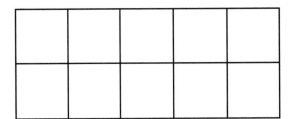

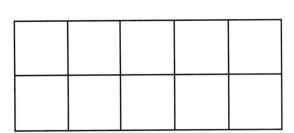

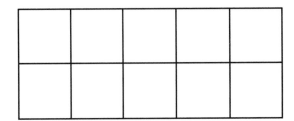

Spin for Beans at Home

H⊙m℮w⊙rk

Dear Family Member:

Your child has played the game *Spin for Beans 100* in school and is ready to teach it to someone at home. You may use coins, paper clips, several scraps of paper, or other small counters instead of beans. Please help your child keep a record of the number of minutes he or she plays and the number of people she or he teaches to play the game.

Thank you for your cooperation.

Make a tally mark for each person you teach to play the game.

Tallies _____

Make a tally mark for every five minutes you play the game.

Tallies _____ Total Minutes _____

Parent's Signature _____

Child's Signature _____

Return this sheet to school by _____ .

Name _____ Date _____

50 Chart

Guess My Number

Homework

Dear Family Member:

Your child is learning about locating and placing numbers in intervals. Help your child locate numbers in intervals by playing "Guess My Number." Your child has practiced this game in class. The rules are listed below. We recommend that you use numbers that are between 1 and 20 to start. Thank you for your cooperation.

For two or more players.

Rules:

- Player 1: Selects a number.

  For example, "I am thinking of a number that is

  between _____ and _____ ."

- Player 2: Tries to guess the number Player 1 has selected.

- Player 1: Corrects Player 2's guess by saying either "It is lower" or "It is higher."

- Player 2: Continues to make guesses as Player 1 continues to give out clues.

Play ends when Player 2 guesses the number.

Players can use a calendar, a 100 chart, or a centimeter ruler to help find the number.

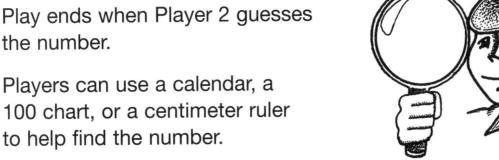

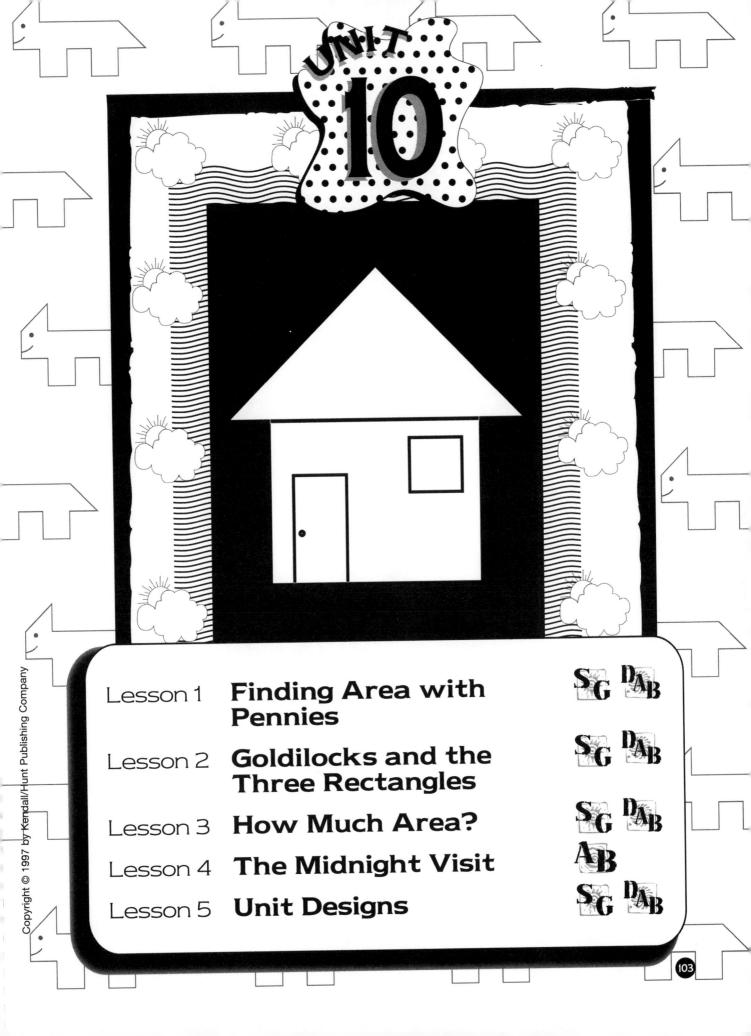

UNIT 10

Lesson 1 **Finding Area with Pennies** S G D A B

Lesson 2 **Goldilocks and the Three Rectangles** S G D A B

Lesson 3 **How Much Area?** S G D A B

Lesson 4 **The Midnight Visit** A B

Lesson 5 **Unit Designs** S G D A B

Draw a Shape

Homework

Dear Family Member:

In class your child measured the area of shapes by counting the number of pennies needed to cover each shape. Please gather pennies and quarters for your child so he or she may have more practice finding area. Help him or her complete the questions below. Thank you.

Draw a large shape in the space below. Then, answer the questions.

1. Cover the shape with pennies. How many cover the shape?

_____

2. Cover the shape with quarters. How many cover the shape?

_____

3. Did more pennies or more quarters fit in the shape? Explain why you think more of this coin fit in the shape.

_____

Rupert Rectangle

Rupert
Rectangle

Square Inches

Unit Designs

Homework

Dear Family Member:

In class your child created a design similar to those below using square-inch and half-square-inch pieces. To find the area of the shapes, your child will count full square inches and piece half-square inches together to make more wholes. Check that your child records the area for each shape and includes the unit of measure, "square inches." Thank you.

Find the area of each of the shapes below. Include in your answer the number and unit.

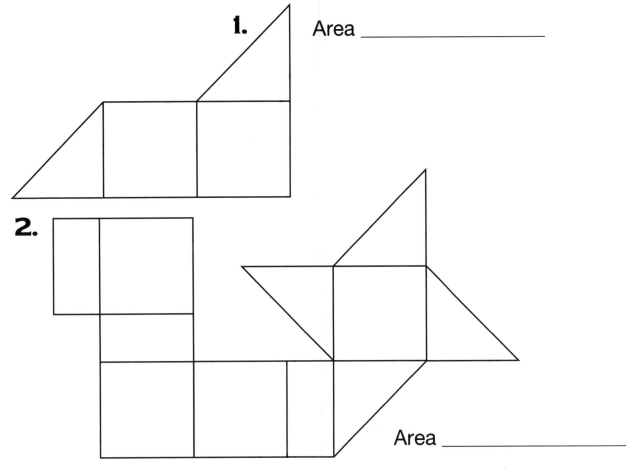

1.   Area _____

2.

Area _____

3.

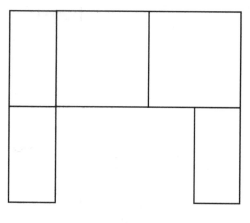

Area _____

4.

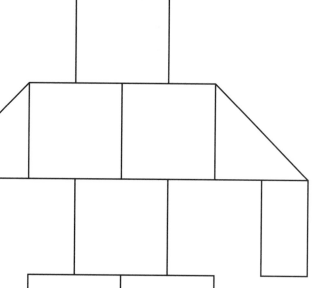

Area _____

Unit Designs

UNIT 11

Lesson 1 **100 Links**

Lesson 2 **Pennies and Dimes**

Lesson 3 **Dimes, Nickels, and Quarters**

Lesson 4 **Arrow Dynamics**

Lesson 5 **How Long Is 100?**

Lesson 6 **Weather 2: Winter Skies**

Lesson 7 **It's Sunny In Arizona**

113

Name _____ Date _____

Starting with 100

Homework

Find the missing numbers. Write two subtraction sentences for each addition sentence. Use the dimes to help you.

90 + __10__ = 100	60 + _____ = 100
100 − 90 = __10__	
100 − __10__ = 90	

_____ + 70 = 100	80 +_____ = 100

Weather 2 Calendar

Time of Day: 🕐   Month: _____   Year: _____

Sunday	Monday	Tuesday	Wednesday	Thursday	Friday	Saturday

Name _____   Date _____

Winter Weather

Which of these items listed below might be important in predicting the weather? Circle the best answer.

A. your grade

C. the number of pets you have

B. where you live

D. the time of year

Below are two graphs. One graph shows data collected in Tucson, Arizona. The other graph shows data collected in Chicago, Illinois. Write the story of each graph in your journal.

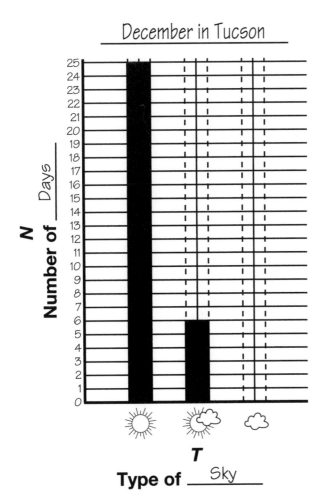

December in Tucson

Number of _Days_   **N**

Type of _Sky_   **T**

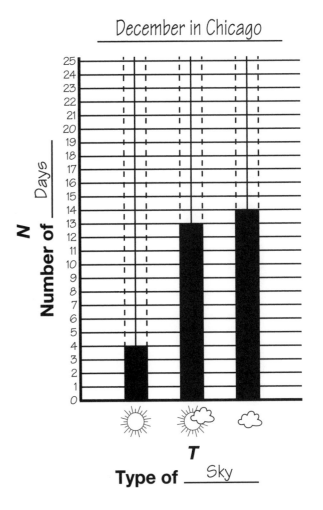

December in Chicago

Number of _Days_   **N**

Type of _Sky_   **T**

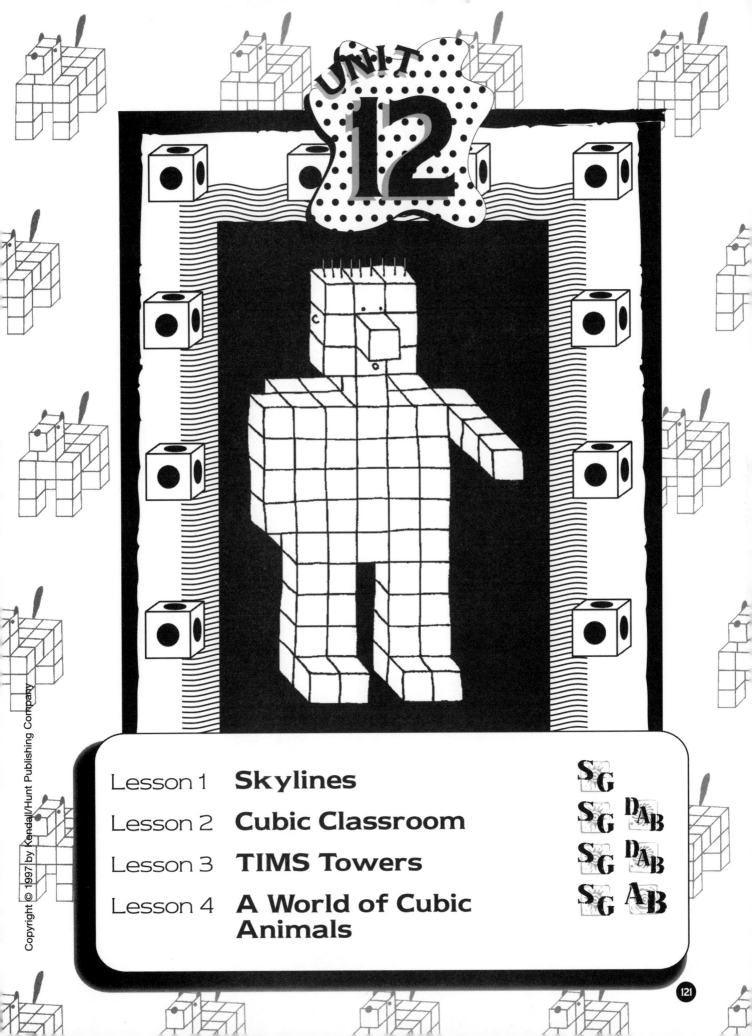

UNIT 12

Lesson 1   **Skylines**   S̲G

Lesson 2   **Cubic Classroom**   S̲G D̲A̲B

Lesson 3   **TIMS Towers**   S̲G D̲A̲B

Lesson 4   **A World of Cubic Animals**   S̲G A̲B

Find and Model Objects

Homework

Find objects in your home that you can model with connecting cubes. The objects should be about the same size as those we modeled in class. Bring an object to school to model with the cubes.

Juice Can

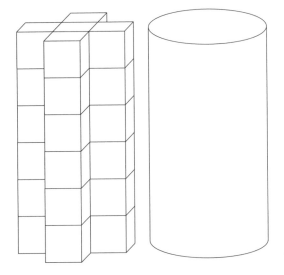

volume of cube model = 30 unit cubes

Name _____   Date _____

Two Towers

Homework

Find the volume of each tower. Then, tell which tower has the greater volume.

Tower 1

Tower 2

Volume = _____   Volume = _____

Which tower has the greater volume? _____

Which tower is the tallest? _____

UNIT 13

I have a 4 card. Do you have a 6 card?

Lesson 1   **Make Ten**

Lesson 2   **Seeing Doubles**

Lesson 3   **Doubles and Halves**

Lesson 4   **Odd and Even Revisited**

Lesson 5   **Problem Solving**

Doubles Bulletin Board

Homework

Dear Family Member:

Your child is studying ways to represent doubling numbers in class.

Things that occur in pairs show doubles: twins, feet, gloves, and shoes. Help your child find or create a picture showing a double number, and help write a number sentence for the picture. An example number sentence for a picture of two feet would be 5 toes + 5 toes = 10 toes.

Thank you for your cooperation.

On this page, draw or paste a cutout picture of a double. Write a number sentence for your double. Bring this page to school for our *Doubles Board*.

Doubles and Halves

Homework

Dear Family Member:

In class your child used connecting cubes to double a number and to find half of a number. For example, to double 6 he or she built a tower with 6 cubes and then doubled it. Your child counted the total number of cubes to find how many cubes were in the new tower. Help your child double and halve the numbers in the table. Your child may use coins, toothpicks, beans, or other counters. Thank you for your cooperation.

Number	The Number Doubled
6	12
10	
14	
17	

Number	Half of Number
8	
26	
38	

Doubles Railroad Game Board

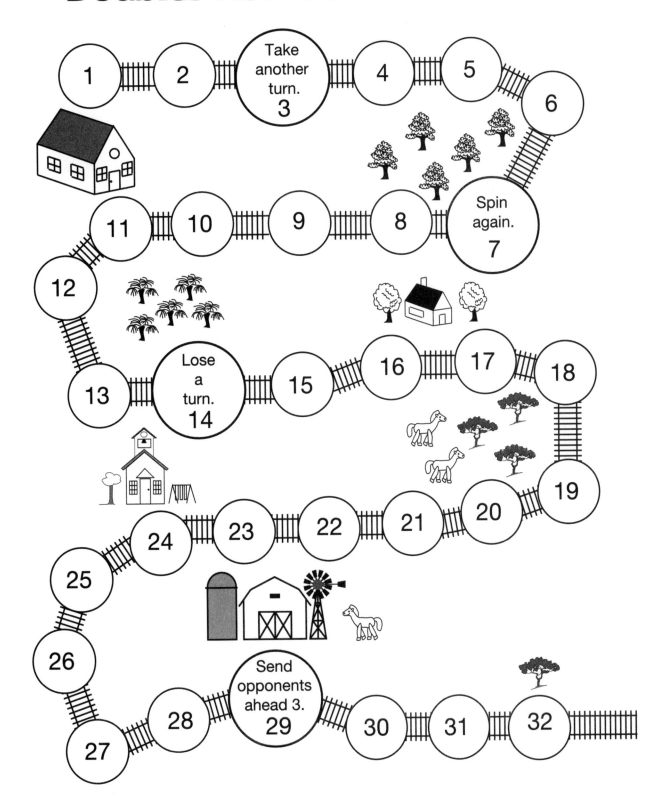

Doubles and Halves

Train
Yard

50

49

48

47

Lose a
turn.
46

45

44

43

Spin
again.
42

41

40

39

38

37

33

34

35

36

Doubles and Halves

Doubles Railroad at Home

Homework

Dear Family Member:

Your child played the game *Doubles Railroad* in school and is ready to teach it to someone at home. Have beans, toothpicks, or other small objects handy for your child to use in solving problems that arise during the game. For example, to double 12, your child might make two stacks of 12 pennies. He or she might skip count by twos to find the total number of pennies.

Please help your child keep a record of the number of people he or she teaches to play the game. You may make a spinner by spinning a paper clip around a pencil.

Thank you for your cooperation.

Make a tally mark for each person you teach to play the game.

Tallies _____

Make a tally mark for every five minutes you play the game.

Tallies _____   Total minutes _____

Parent's signature _____

Child's signature _____

Return this sheet to school by _____ .

Recipe for Peanut Butter, Jelly, and Banana Sandwiches

For One Class

20 slices of bread	**10 tablespoons of jelly**
4 bananas	**10 tablespoons of peanut butter**

1. Pretend you need to serve sandwiches to two classes. How many of each ingredient will you need to double the recipe?

_____ slices of bread   _____ tablespoons of jelly

_____ bananas   _____ tablespoons of peanut butter

2. Pretend you need to serve sandwiches to only half the class. How many of each ingredient will you need to make only half the recipe?

_____ slices of bread   _____ tablespoons of jelly

_____ bananas   _____ tablespoons of peanut butter

Lesson 1   **Math Mice**   SG

Lesson 2   **Pets**   SG

Lesson 3   **Problems that Will Knock Your Socks Off!**   SG

Note: The student pages for this Unit may be found in the *Student Guide*.

UNIT 15

Lesson 1   **Tubes, Boxes, Spheres, and Cubes**   S G

Lesson 2   **Sizing Cylinders**   S G D A B

Lesson 3   **Looking at Prisms**   S G D A B

Lesson 4   **In the Shapes Kitchen**   U R G

Box Collection

Homework

Dear Family Member:

In school, we will study boxes to learn about the shape properties of cubes and rectangular prisms (boxes). I have asked your child to look at home for boxes to use in a class activity. Please help your child find and select one or two boxes to bring to school.

Thank you for your cooperation.

Our class needs a box collection. Look at home for one or two boxes to bring to school tomorrow. Here are a few examples:

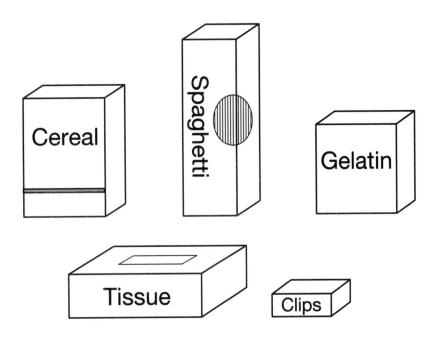

Box Measurements

Work with a partner to measure the length of each face of
your box. First, use a metric ruler to measure the length one
way. Then, measure the length another way. Record the
measurements in the table below.

Box Measurement Data Table

Faces of the Box	Length One Way (in centimeters)	Length Another Way (in centimeters)
Face 1		
Face 2		
Face 3		
Face 4		
Face 5		
Face 6		

Homework

Dear Family Member:

In class, your child has explored various three-dimensional shapes in their environment. I have asked your child to find everyday objects at home that have a spherical (ball) shape. Your child should record his or her findings in the data table on the back of this page. Please help your child find examples.

I have also asked your child to bring food ads to school. I am most interested in ads that show pictures or drawings of food containers, such as boxes and cans, or produce, such as oranges and cucumbers. As a class activity, your child will create a book with cutouts of these geometric shapes.

Thank you for your cooperation.

Sphere Search

Search for objects that have a sphere shape. Then, record the names of the sphere shapes you see at your home in the data table on the back of this page. Make the headings in your data table look like the ones below.

Sphere Shape	Almost Sphere Shape

Bring food ads to school.

UNIT 16

Lesson 1   **The Martians**

Lesson 2   **Food Sort**

Lesson 3   **Healthy Kids**

Homework

Favorite Foods

List ten of your favorite foods.

1. _____

2. _____

3. _____

4. _____

5. _____

6. _____

7. _____

8. _____

9. _____

10. _____

Joni's and Bobbie's Breakfasts

Homework

Joni eats the same breakfast every day. She eats rice puffs, milk, slices of apples, and banana bread.

Bobbie also eats the same breakfast every day. She eats a Belgian waffle with strawberries, whipped cream, and maple syrup, bacon, and a glass of milk.

Help them find out what food groups their breakfast foods belong to. Write the number(s) of the food group(s) after each food.

Joni's Breakfast

milk _____

banana bread _____

rice puffs _____

slices of apples _____

Bobbie's Breakfast

Belgian waffle _____

strawberries _____

whipped cream _____

maple syrup _____

bacon _____

1. **Bread, Cereal, Rice, and Pasta Group**

2. **Vegetable Group**

3. **Fruit Group**

4. **Milk, Yogurt, and Cheese Group**

5. **Meat, Poultry, Fish, Dry Beans, Eggs, and Nuts Group**

6. **Fats, Oils, and Sweets**

David's and Cindy's Food

1. Use the tallies to find the total number of servings for each food group that David and Cindy ate in one day.

David's Data Table

Food Group	Tallies	Total
bread, etc.	|||	
vegetables	|||	
fruits	|||	
milk, etc.	|||	
meat, etc.	|||	
fats/sweets	|||	

Cindy's Data Table

Food Group	Tallies	Total
bread, etc.	||	
vegetables	||||	
fruits	|||	
milk, etc.	|	
meat, etc.	|||	
fats/sweets	|	

2. Compare the data in David's and Cindy's data tables.

A. Who ate more bread, cereal, rice, and pasta? How much more?

_____

_____

_____

B. Who ate more servings of food in one day? How many more servings?

_____

_____

_____

C. Make up your own problem based on the two data tables. Then, show how to find the answer.

_____

_____

_____

Name _____ Date _____

3. Transfer the data from David's data table to David's graph.

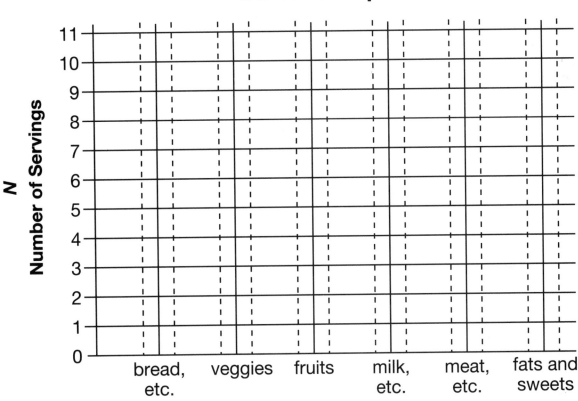

David's Graph

N
Number of Servings
11, 10, 9, 8, 7, 6, 5, 4, 3, 2, 1, 0

bread, etc.   veggies   fruits   milk, etc.   meat, etc.   fats and sweets

G
Food Group

4. Tell the story of David's graph. What do you think about David's diet? What should he keep the same? What should he change?

_____

_____

_____

UNIT 17

Lesson 1	**Tensland**	**A** **B**
Lesson 2	**Our Class in Tensland**	**S** **G** **D** **A** **B**
Lesson 3	**Counting One Hundred Seventy-two**	**S** **G**
Lesson 4	**Adding Hundreds**	**S** **G** **D** **A** **B**

At Home in Tensland

Homework

Dear Family Member:

At school, your child has been working on counting and grouping large numbers of objects. You can help your child share with you what he or she has learned. Please provide your child with a large number (more than 100 but less than 200) of objects to count. Some suggestions for objects: toothpicks, paper clips, macaroni, beans, small screws, washers/hex nuts, or pennies. Also, have small cups or containers available for sorting. Your child will then illustrate how the objects were counted and record the total number.

Thank you for your cooperation.

Report on what you counted at home:

1. The kind of objects I counted at home were:

_____

2. My drawing below shows how I counted the objects.

3. I write that number of objects as _____ .

Terry in Tensland

Terry also visited Tensland. He met a bunch of beans. They wanted help to get organized. Terry put them into groups of two to make them easier to count.

Terrry counted 116 beans.

Do you agree with his count? _____

Tell Terry how to organize the beans another way.

_____

More Adding Numbers

Homework

Show your thinking for solving each set of problems below.
Then, share your work with a family member.

Set 1

4 + 3 = _____   40 + 30 = _____   400 + 300 = _____

Set 2

$$\begin{array}{r} 5 \\ + 3 \\ \hline \end{array}$$
$$\begin{array}{r} 50 \\ + 30 \\ \hline \end{array}$$
$$\begin{array}{r} 500 \\ + 300 \\ \hline \end{array}$$

Set 3

$$\begin{array}{r} 6 \\ 1 \\ + 2 \\ \hline \end{array}$$
$$\begin{array}{r} 60 \\ 10 \\ + 20 \\ \hline \end{array}$$
$$\begin{array}{r} 600 \\ 100 \\ + 200 \\ \hline \end{array}$$

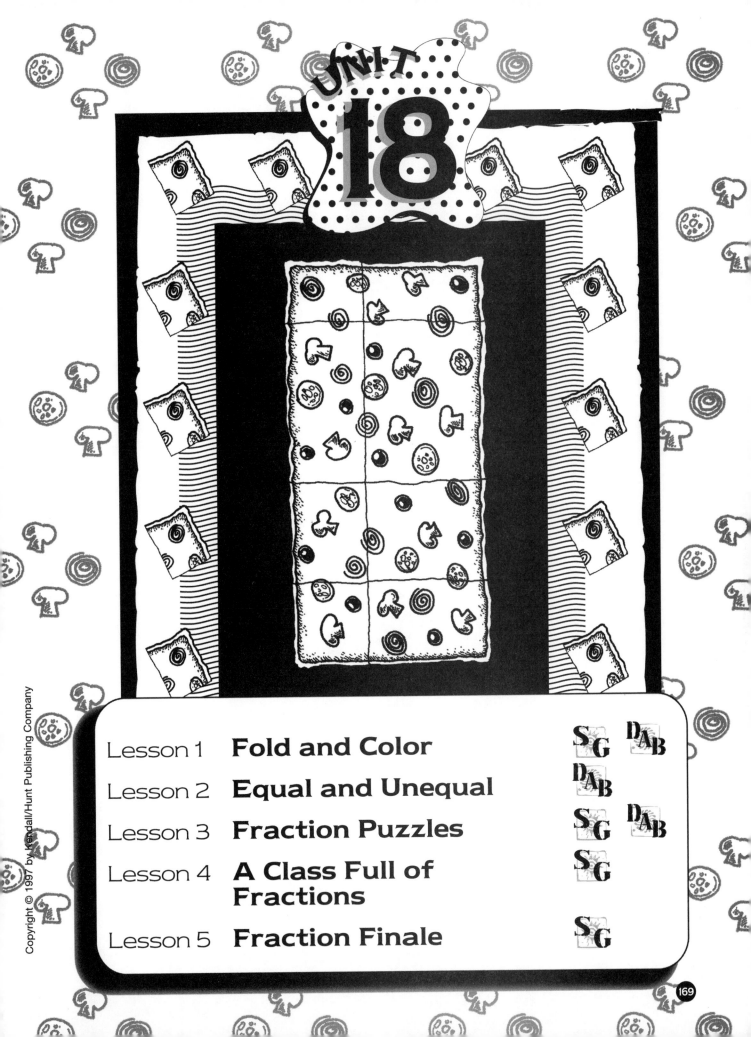

UNIT 18

Lesson 1 **Fold and Color** $\text{S}{G}$ $\text{D}{AB}$

Lesson 2 **Equal and Unequal** $\text{D}{AB}$

Lesson 3 **Fraction Puzzles** $\text{S}{G}$ $\text{D}{AB}$

Lesson 4 **A Class Full of Fractions** $\text{S}{G}$

Lesson 5 **Fraction Finale** $\text{S}{G}$

Name _____ Date _____

Fold and Color 1

Cut out the shapes below. Use them to complete the *Folding and Showing Halves* Activity Pages in your Student Guide.

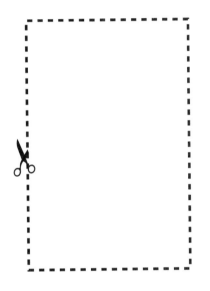

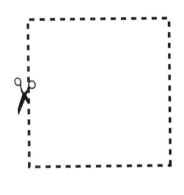

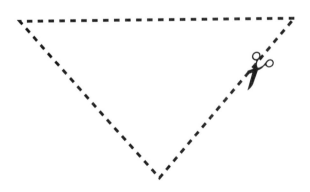

Fold and Color 2

Cut out the shapes below. Use them to complete the *Folding and Showing Fourths* Activity Pages in your Student Guide.

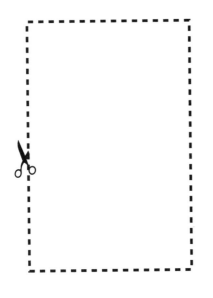

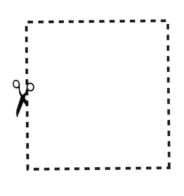

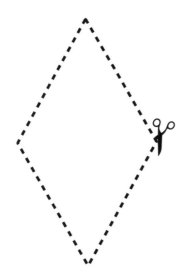

Halves and Fourths in My Home

Homework

Dear Family Member:

In class today, we were exploring the concepts of halves and fourths. We have asked your child to look at home for six items that come in halves or fourths. Please help him or her complete this task. Some suggestions follow:

- A cracker might be scored to break easily into halves or fourths.
- Milk is packaged in one-half gallon and one-fourth gallon (quart) containers.
- One pound of butter or margarine is often divided into one-quarter pound sticks.

If your child cannot find six items, help him or her complete the list below by adding items, such as paper towels or napkins, that can easily be folded or cut in halves or fourths. If possible, have your child bring one example to school to share with the class.

Thank you for your cooperation.

Look around your home for six items that come in fourths or halves. Make a list of them below.

1. _____   2. _____

3. _____   4. _____

5. _____   6. _____

To Halve and to Halve Not

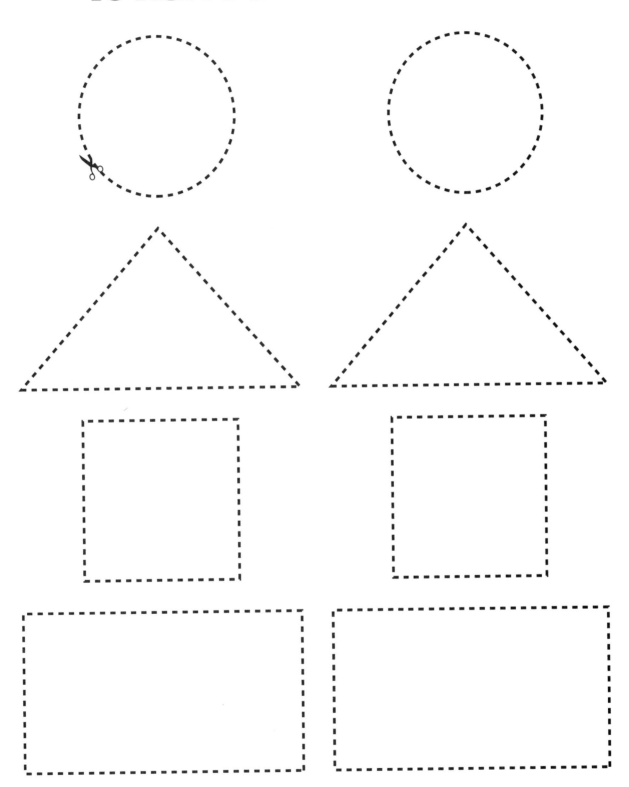

To Fourth and to Fourth Not

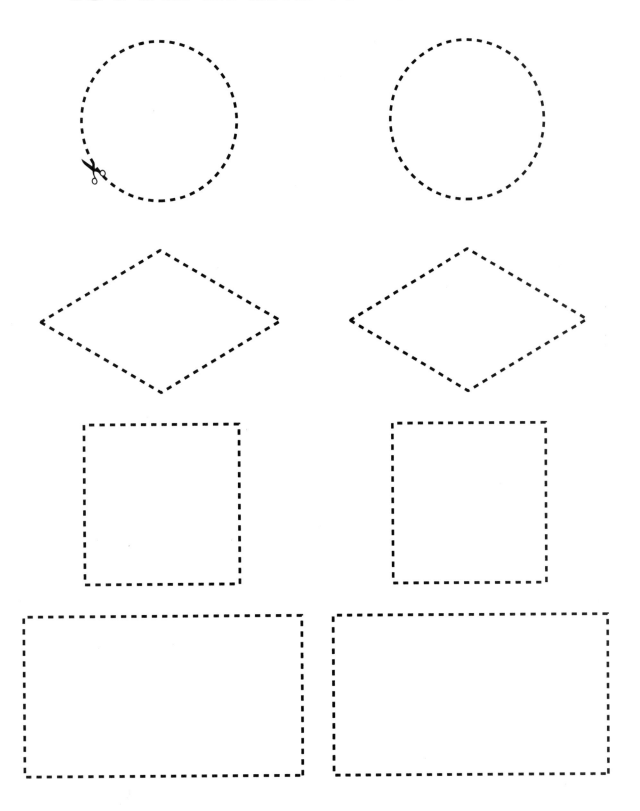

Equal and Unequal Unit 18 · Lesson 2 **179**

Circles and Ovals

Rectangles and Squares

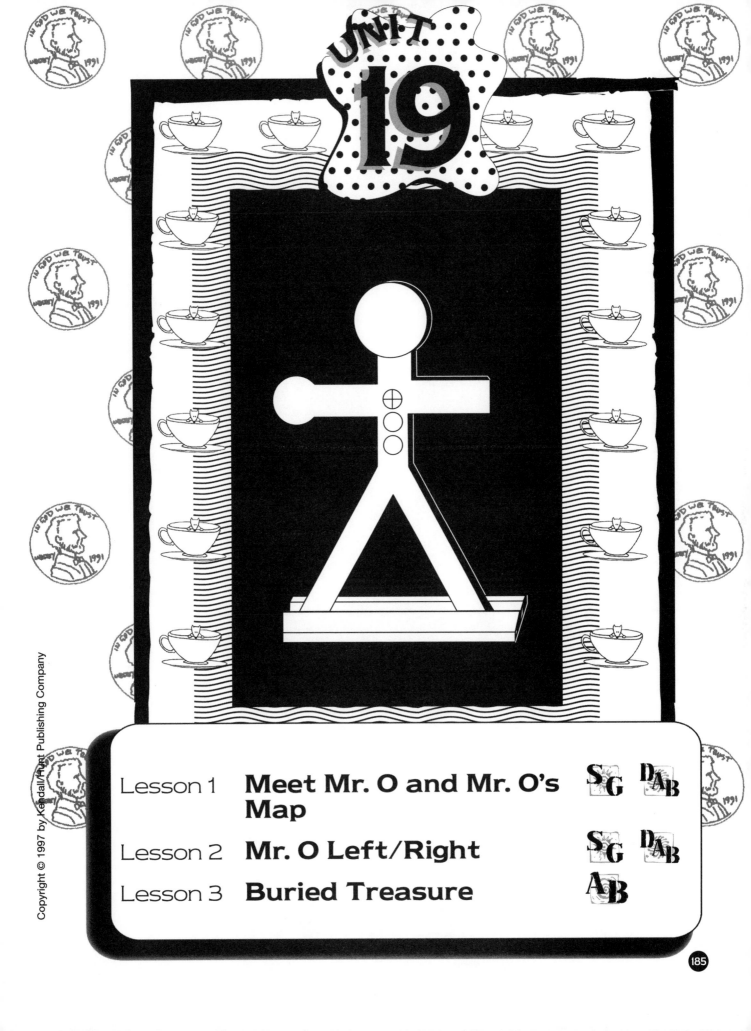

Lesson 1   **Meet Mr. O and Mr. O's Map**   S G   D A B

Lesson 2   **Mr. O Left/Right**   S G   D A B

Lesson 3   **Buried Treasure**   A B

185

Mr. O Says

Homework

Dear Family Member:

In class today, we used a plastic figure called Mr. O to help develop skills in understanding the directions right/left and front/back. Your child would like to share this learning experience with you. The hand with the circular mitten is Mr. O's right hand. The buttons show that we are looking at Mr. O's front side. Help your child cut out Mr. O below. Then, follow the directions and play *Mr. O Says* with your child.

Thank you for your cooperation.

1. Cut out Mr. O. Make sure the mitten on Mr. O's right hand is easy to see.

2. Decide who will be Mr. O, you or your family member.

3. One player makes a statement such as, "The refrigerator is to my right."

4. The Mr. O player moves Mr. O to make the statement true.

5. Reverse roles after you play a few rounds.

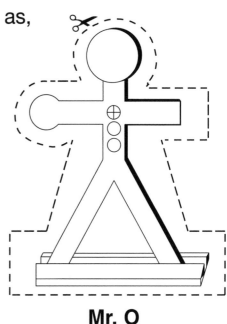

Mr. O

Here are a few more statements you might use to get started.

Mr. O says, "The chair is below me."
Mr. O says, "The door is in front of me."
Mr. O says, "The stove is to my right."
Now you are ready to play *Mr. O Says!*

Name _____ Date _____

Map

Make a map of your Mr. O lab setup. Number the line by 2's. Then, show the location of the objects. Put a *T* for 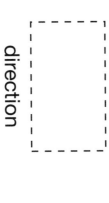, an *S* for ◇, an *R* for ◇, and an *H* for ⬡.

0

_____
unit

┌─ ─ ─ ─ ─┐
│   │
│   │
└─ ─ ─ ─ ─┘
direction

┌─ ─ ─ ─ ─┐
│   │
│   │
└─ ─ ─ ─ ─┘
direction

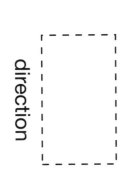

UNIT 20

Lesson 1   **Problem Solving**

Lesson 2   **End-of-Year Test**

Note: The student pages for this Unit may be found in the *Student Guide* and the *Unit Resource Guide*.